Wine Name ____________________

Winery ____________ Region ____________

Grapes ____________ Vintage ____________ Alcohol % ________

Appearance		☆ ☆ ☆ ☆ ☆
Aroma		☆ ☆ ☆ ☆ ☆
Body		☆ ☆ ☆ ☆ ☆
Taste		☆ ☆ ☆ ☆ ☆
Finish		☆ ☆ ☆ ☆ ☆

Pairs With	Serving Temperature

Notes

Ratings ☆ ☆ ☆ ☆ ☆

Wine Name

Winery ______________ Region ______________

Grapes ______________ Vintage ______________ Alcohol % ______________

Appearance		☆ ☆ ☆ ☆ ☆
Aroma		☆ ☆ ☆ ☆ ☆
Body		☆ ☆ ☆ ☆ ☆
Taste		☆ ☆ ☆ ☆ ☆
Finish		☆ ☆ ☆ ☆ ☆

Pairs With	Serving Temperature

Notes

Ratings ☆ ☆ ☆ ☆ ☆

Wine Name ______________________

Winery ______________ Region ______________

Grapes ______________ Vintage ______________ Alcohol % __________

Appearance		☆ ☆ ☆ ☆ ☆
Aroma		☆ ☆ ☆ ☆ ☆
Body		☆ ☆ ☆ ☆ ☆
Taste		☆ ☆ ☆ ☆ ☆
Finish		☆ ☆ ☆ ☆ ☆

Pairs With	Serving Temperature

Notes

Ratings ☆ ☆ ☆ ☆ ☆

Wine Name

Winery ______________ Region ______________

Grapes ______________ Vintage ______________ Alcohol % __________

Appearance		☆ ☆ ☆ ☆ ☆
Aroma		☆ ☆ ☆ ☆ ☆
Body		☆ ☆ ☆ ☆ ☆
Taste		☆ ☆ ☆ ☆ ☆
Finish		☆ ☆ ☆ ☆ ☆

Pairs With	Serving Temperature

Notes

Ratings ☆ ☆ ☆ ☆ ☆

Wine Name ____________________

Winery ____________ Region ____________

Grapes ____________ Vintage ____________ Alcohol % ________

Appearance		☆ ☆ ☆ ☆ ☆
Aroma		☆ ☆ ☆ ☆ ☆
Body		☆ ☆ ☆ ☆ ☆
Taste		☆ ☆ ☆ ☆ ☆
Finish		☆ ☆ ☆ ☆ ☆

Pairs With	Serving Temperature

Notes

Ratings ☆ ☆ ☆ ☆ ☆

Wine Name ____________________

Winery ____________ Region ____________

Grapes ____________ Vintage ____________ Alcohol % ________

Appearance		☆ ☆ ☆ ☆ ☆
Aroma		☆ ☆ ☆ ☆ ☆
Body		☆ ☆ ☆ ☆ ☆
Taste		☆ ☆ ☆ ☆ ☆
Finish		☆ ☆ ☆ ☆ ☆

Pairs With	Serving Temperature

Notes

Ratings ☆ ☆ ☆ ☆ ☆

Wine Name ____________________

Winery __________ Region __________

Grapes __________ Vintage __________ Alcohol % ______

Appearance		☆ ☆ ☆ ☆ ☆
Aroma		☆ ☆ ☆ ☆ ☆
Body		☆ ☆ ☆ ☆ ☆
Taste		☆ ☆ ☆ ☆ ☆
Finish		☆ ☆ ☆ ☆ ☆

Pairs With	Serving Temperature

Notes

Ratings ☆ ☆ ☆ ☆ ☆

Wine Name

Winery ____________ Region ____________

Grapes ____________ Vintage ____________ Alcohol % ____________

Appearance		☆ ☆ ☆ ☆ ☆
Aroma		☆ ☆ ☆ ☆ ☆
Body		☆ ☆ ☆ ☆ ☆
Taste		☆ ☆ ☆ ☆ ☆
Finish		☆ ☆ ☆ ☆ ☆

Pairs With	Serving Temperature

Notes

Ratings ☆ ☆ ☆ ☆ ☆

Wine Name

Winery ____________ Region ____________

Grapes ____________ Vintage ____________ Alcohol % ____________

Appearance		☆ ☆ ☆ ☆ ☆
Aroma		☆ ☆ ☆ ☆ ☆
Body		☆ ☆ ☆ ☆ ☆
Taste		☆ ☆ ☆ ☆ ☆
Finish		☆ ☆ ☆ ☆ ☆

Pairs With	Serving Temperature

Notes

Ratings ☆ ☆ ☆ ☆ ☆

Wine Name ______________________

Winery ______________ Region ______________

Grapes ______________ Vintage ______________ Alcohol % ________

Appearance		☆ ☆ ☆ ☆ ☆
Aroma		☆ ☆ ☆ ☆ ☆
Body		☆ ☆ ☆ ☆ ☆
Taste		☆ ☆ ☆ ☆ ☆
Finish		☆ ☆ ☆ ☆ ☆

Pairs With	Serving Temperature

Notes

Ratings ☆ ☆ ☆ ☆ ☆

Wine Name ______________________

Winery ____________ Region ____________

Grapes ____________ Vintage ____________ Alcohol % ________

Appearance		☆ ☆ ☆ ☆ ☆
Aroma		☆ ☆ ☆ ☆ ☆
Body		☆ ☆ ☆ ☆ ☆
Taste		☆ ☆ ☆ ☆ ☆
Finish		☆ ☆ ☆ ☆ ☆

Pairs With	Serving Temperature

Notes

Ratings ☆ ☆ ☆ ☆ ☆

Wine Name ____________________

Winery ____________ Region ____________

Grapes ____________ Vintage ____________ Alcohol % ________

Appearance		☆ ☆ ☆ ☆ ☆
Aroma		☆ ☆ ☆ ☆ ☆
Body		☆ ☆ ☆ ☆ ☆
Taste		☆ ☆ ☆ ☆ ☆
Finish		☆ ☆ ☆ ☆ ☆

Pairs With	Serving Temperature

Notes

Ratings ☆ ☆ ☆ ☆ ☆

Wine Name

Winery ________ Region ________

Grapes ________ Vintage ________ Alcohol % ________

Appearance		☆ ☆ ☆ ☆ ☆
Aroma		☆ ☆ ☆ ☆ ☆
Body		☆ ☆ ☆ ☆ ☆
Taste		☆ ☆ ☆ ☆ ☆
Finish		☆ ☆ ☆ ☆ ☆

Pairs With	Serving Temperature

Notes

Ratings ☆ ☆ ☆ ☆ ☆

Wine Name

Winery ______ Region ______

Grapes ______ Vintage ______ Alcohol % ______

Appearance		☆ ☆ ☆ ☆ ☆
Aroma		☆ ☆ ☆ ☆ ☆
Body		☆ ☆ ☆ ☆ ☆
Taste		☆ ☆ ☆ ☆ ☆
Finish		☆ ☆ ☆ ☆ ☆

Pairs With	Serving Temperature

Notes

Ratings ☆ ☆ ☆ ☆ ☆

Wine Name ______________________

Winery ____________ Region ____________

Grapes ____________ Vintage ____________ Alcohol % ________

Appearance		☆ ☆ ☆ ☆ ☆
Aroma		☆ ☆ ☆ ☆ ☆
Body		☆ ☆ ☆ ☆ ☆
Taste		☆ ☆ ☆ ☆ ☆
Finish		☆ ☆ ☆ ☆ ☆

Pairs With	Serving Temperature

Notes

Ratings ☆ ☆ ☆ ☆ ☆

Wine Name

Winery

Region

Grapes

Vintage

Alcohol %

Appearance		☆ ☆ ☆ ☆ ☆
Aroma		☆ ☆ ☆ ☆ ☆
Body		☆ ☆ ☆ ☆ ☆
Taste		☆ ☆ ☆ ☆ ☆
Finish		☆ ☆ ☆ ☆ ☆

Pairs With

Serving Temperature

Notes

Ratings ☆ ☆ ☆ ☆ ☆

Wine Name

Winery Region

Grapes Vintage Alcohol %

Appearance		☆ ☆ ☆ ☆ ☆
Aroma		☆ ☆ ☆ ☆ ☆
Body		☆ ☆ ☆ ☆ ☆
Taste		☆ ☆ ☆ ☆ ☆
Finish		☆ ☆ ☆ ☆ ☆

Pairs With

Serving Temperature

Notes

Ratings ☆ ☆ ☆ ☆ ☆

Wine Name ______________________

Winery ______________ Region ______________

Grapes ______________ Vintage ______________ Alcohol % ________

Appearance		☆ ☆ ☆ ☆ ☆
Aroma		☆ ☆ ☆ ☆ ☆
Body		☆ ☆ ☆ ☆ ☆
Taste		☆ ☆ ☆ ☆ ☆
Finish		☆ ☆ ☆ ☆ ☆

Pairs With	Serving Temperature

Notes

Ratings ☆ ☆ ☆ ☆ ☆

Wine Name ______________________

Winery ____________ Region ____________

Grapes ____________ Vintage ____________ Alcohol % ________

Appearance		☆ ☆ ☆ ☆ ☆
Aroma		☆ ☆ ☆ ☆ ☆
Body		☆ ☆ ☆ ☆ ☆
Taste		☆ ☆ ☆ ☆ ☆
Finish		☆ ☆ ☆ ☆ ☆

Pairs With	Serving Temperature

Notes

Ratings ☆ ☆ ☆ ☆ ☆

Wine Name

Winery ____________ Region ____________

Grapes ____________ Vintage ____________ Alcohol % ____________

Appearance		☆ ☆ ☆ ☆ ☆
Aroma		☆ ☆ ☆ ☆ ☆
Body		☆ ☆ ☆ ☆ ☆
Taste		☆ ☆ ☆ ☆ ☆
Finish		☆ ☆ ☆ ☆ ☆

Pairs With	Serving Temperature

Notes

Ratings ☆ ☆ ☆ ☆ ☆

Wine Name

Winery

Region

Grapes

Vintage

Alcohol %

Appearance		☆ ☆ ☆ ☆ ☆
Aroma		☆ ☆ ☆ ☆ ☆
Body		☆ ☆ ☆ ☆ ☆
Taste		☆ ☆ ☆ ☆ ☆
Finish		☆ ☆ ☆ ☆ ☆

Pairs With

Serving Temperature

Notes

Ratings ☆ ☆ ☆ ☆ ☆

Wine Name

Winery ____________ Region ____________

Grapes ____________ Vintage ____________ Alcohol % ____________

Appearance		☆ ☆ ☆ ☆ ☆
Aroma		☆ ☆ ☆ ☆ ☆
Body		☆ ☆ ☆ ☆ ☆
Taste		☆ ☆ ☆ ☆ ☆
Finish		☆ ☆ ☆ ☆ ☆

Pairs With	Serving Temperature

Notes

Ratings ☆ ☆ ☆ ☆ ☆

Wine Name ______________________

Winery ____________ Region ____________

Grapes ____________ Vintage ____________ Alcohol % ________

Appearance		☆ ☆ ☆ ☆ ☆
Aroma		☆ ☆ ☆ ☆ ☆
Body		☆ ☆ ☆ ☆ ☆
Taste		☆ ☆ ☆ ☆ ☆
Finish		☆ ☆ ☆ ☆ ☆

Pairs With	Serving Temperature

Notes

Ratings ☆ ☆ ☆ ☆ ☆

Wine Name ______________________

Winery ______________ Region ______________

Grapes ______________ Vintage ______________ Alcohol % ________

Appearance		☆ ☆ ☆ ☆ ☆
Aroma		☆ ☆ ☆ ☆ ☆
Body		☆ ☆ ☆ ☆ ☆
Taste		☆ ☆ ☆ ☆ ☆
Finish		☆ ☆ ☆ ☆ ☆

Pairs With	Serving Temperature

Notes

Ratings ☆ ☆ ☆ ☆ ☆

Wine Name

Winery ______ Region ______

Grapes ______ Vintage ______ Alcohol % ______

Appearance		☆ ☆ ☆ ☆ ☆
Aroma		☆ ☆ ☆ ☆ ☆
Body		☆ ☆ ☆ ☆ ☆
Taste		☆ ☆ ☆ ☆ ☆
Finish		☆ ☆ ☆ ☆ ☆

Pairs With	Serving Temperature

Notes

Ratings ☆ ☆ ☆ ☆ ☆

Wine Name ____________________

Winery ____________ Region ____________

Grapes ____________ Vintage ____________ Alcohol % ________

Appearance		☆ ☆ ☆ ☆ ☆
Aroma		☆ ☆ ☆ ☆ ☆
Body		☆ ☆ ☆ ☆ ☆
Taste		☆ ☆ ☆ ☆ ☆
Finish		☆ ☆ ☆ ☆ ☆

Pairs With	Serving Temperature

Notes

Ratings ☆ ☆ ☆ ☆ ☆

Wine Name

Winery ______ Region ______

Grapes ______ Vintage ______ Alcohol % ______

Appearance		☆ ☆ ☆ ☆ ☆
Aroma		☆ ☆ ☆ ☆ ☆
Body		☆ ☆ ☆ ☆ ☆
Taste		☆ ☆ ☆ ☆ ☆
Finish		☆ ☆ ☆ ☆ ☆

Pairs With	Serving Temperature

Notes

Ratings ☆ ☆ ☆ ☆ ☆

Wine Name ______________________

Winery ______________ Region ______________

Grapes ______________ Vintage ______________ Alcohol % ________

Appearance		☆ ☆ ☆ ☆ ☆
Aroma		☆ ☆ ☆ ☆ ☆
Body		☆ ☆ ☆ ☆ ☆
Taste		☆ ☆ ☆ ☆ ☆
Finish		☆ ☆ ☆ ☆ ☆

Pairs With	Serving Temperature

Notes

Ratings ☆ ☆ ☆ ☆ ☆

Wine Name ____________________

Winery ____________ Region ____________

Grapes ____________ Vintage ____________ Alcohol % ________

Appearance		☆ ☆ ☆ ☆ ☆
Aroma		☆ ☆ ☆ ☆ ☆
Body		☆ ☆ ☆ ☆ ☆
Taste		☆ ☆ ☆ ☆ ☆
Finish		☆ ☆ ☆ ☆ ☆

Pairs With	Serving Temperature

Notes

Ratings ☆ ☆ ☆ ☆ ☆

Wine Name

Winery ____________ Region ____________

Grapes ____________ Vintage ____________ Alcohol % ____________

Appearance		☆ ☆ ☆ ☆ ☆
Aroma		☆ ☆ ☆ ☆ ☆
Body		☆ ☆ ☆ ☆ ☆
Taste		☆ ☆ ☆ ☆ ☆
Finish		☆ ☆ ☆ ☆ ☆

Pairs With	Serving Temperature

Notes

Ratings ☆ ☆ ☆ ☆ ☆

Wine Name ______________________

Winery ______________ Region ______________

Grapes ______________ Vintage ______________ Alcohol % ________

Appearance		☆ ☆ ☆ ☆ ☆
Aroma		☆ ☆ ☆ ☆ ☆
Body		☆ ☆ ☆ ☆ ☆
Taste		☆ ☆ ☆ ☆ ☆
Finish		☆ ☆ ☆ ☆ ☆

Pairs With	Serving Temperature

Notes

Ratings ☆ ☆ ☆ ☆ ☆

Wine Name ____________________

Winery ____________ Region ____________

Grapes ____________ Vintage ____________ Alcohol % ________

Appearance		☆ ☆ ☆ ☆ ☆
Aroma		☆ ☆ ☆ ☆ ☆
Body		☆ ☆ ☆ ☆ ☆
Taste		☆ ☆ ☆ ☆ ☆
Finish		☆ ☆ ☆ ☆ ☆

Pairs With	Serving Temperature

Notes

Ratings ☆ ☆ ☆ ☆ ☆

Wine Name

Winery ______________ Region ______________

Grapes ______________ Vintage ______________ Alcohol % __________

Appearance		☆ ☆ ☆ ☆ ☆
Aroma		☆ ☆ ☆ ☆ ☆
Body		☆ ☆ ☆ ☆ ☆
Taste		☆ ☆ ☆ ☆ ☆
Finish		☆ ☆ ☆ ☆ ☆

Pairs With	Serving Temperature

Notes

Ratings ☆ ☆ ☆ ☆ ☆

Wine Name ______________________

Winery ____________ Region ____________

Grapes ____________ Vintage ____________ Alcohol % ________

Appearance		☆ ☆ ☆ ☆ ☆
Aroma		☆ ☆ ☆ ☆ ☆
Body		☆ ☆ ☆ ☆ ☆
Taste		☆ ☆ ☆ ☆ ☆
Finish		☆ ☆ ☆ ☆ ☆

Pairs With	Serving Temperature

Notes

Ratings ☆ ☆ ☆ ☆ ☆

Wine Name

Winery

Region

Grapes

Vintage

Alcohol %

Appearance		☆ ☆ ☆ ☆ ☆
Aroma		☆ ☆ ☆ ☆ ☆
Body		☆ ☆ ☆ ☆ ☆
Taste		☆ ☆ ☆ ☆ ☆
Finish		☆ ☆ ☆ ☆ ☆

Pairs With	Serving Temperature

Notes

Ratings ☆ ☆ ☆ ☆ ☆

Wine Name

Winery ____________ Region ____________

Grapes ____________ Vintage ____________ Alcohol % ____________

Appearance		☆ ☆ ☆ ☆ ☆
Aroma		☆ ☆ ☆ ☆ ☆
Body		☆ ☆ ☆ ☆ ☆
Taste		☆ ☆ ☆ ☆ ☆
Finish		☆ ☆ ☆ ☆ ☆

Pairs With	Serving Temperature

Notes

Ratings ☆ ☆ ☆ ☆ ☆

Wine Name ______________________

Winery ____________ Region ____________

Grapes ____________ Vintage ____________ Alcohol % ________

Appearance		☆ ☆ ☆ ☆ ☆
Aroma		☆ ☆ ☆ ☆ ☆
Body		☆ ☆ ☆ ☆ ☆
Taste		☆ ☆ ☆ ☆ ☆
Finish		☆ ☆ ☆ ☆ ☆

Pairs With	Serving Temperature

Notes

Ratings ☆ ☆ ☆ ☆ ☆

Wine Name ____________________

Winery __________ Region __________

Grapes __________ Vintage __________ Alcohol % ______

Appearance		☆ ☆ ☆ ☆ ☆
Aroma		☆ ☆ ☆ ☆ ☆
Body		☆ ☆ ☆ ☆ ☆
Taste		☆ ☆ ☆ ☆ ☆
Finish		☆ ☆ ☆ ☆ ☆

Pairs With	Serving Temperature

Notes

Ratings ☆ ☆ ☆ ☆ ☆

Wine Name ____________________

Winery ____________ Region ____________

Grapes ____________ Vintage ____________ Alcohol % ________

Appearance		☆ ☆ ☆ ☆ ☆
Aroma		☆ ☆ ☆ ☆ ☆
Body		☆ ☆ ☆ ☆ ☆
Taste		☆ ☆ ☆ ☆ ☆
Finish		☆ ☆ ☆ ☆ ☆

Pairs With	Serving Temperature

Notes

Ratings ☆ ☆ ☆ ☆ ☆

Wine Name ______________________

Winery ______________ Region ______________

Grapes ______________ Vintage ______________ Alcohol % __________

Appearance		☆ ☆ ☆ ☆ ☆
Aroma		☆ ☆ ☆ ☆ ☆
Body		☆ ☆ ☆ ☆ ☆
Taste		☆ ☆ ☆ ☆ ☆
Finish		☆ ☆ ☆ ☆ ☆

Pairs With	Serving Temperature

Notes

Ratings ☆ ☆ ☆ ☆ ☆

Wine Name

Winery ______________ Region ______________

Grapes ______________ Vintage ______________ Alcohol % ______________

Appearance		☆ ☆ ☆ ☆ ☆
Aroma		☆ ☆ ☆ ☆ ☆
Body		☆ ☆ ☆ ☆ ☆
Taste		☆ ☆ ☆ ☆ ☆
Finish		☆ ☆ ☆ ☆ ☆

Pairs With	Serving Temperature

Notes

Ratings ☆ ☆ ☆ ☆ ☆

Wine Name

Winery | Region

Grapes | Vintage | Alcohol %

Appearance		☆ ☆ ☆ ☆ ☆
Aroma		☆ ☆ ☆ ☆ ☆
Body		☆ ☆ ☆ ☆ ☆
Taste		☆ ☆ ☆ ☆ ☆
Finish		☆ ☆ ☆ ☆ ☆

Pairs With

Serving Temperature

Notes

Ratings ☆ ☆ ☆ ☆ ☆

Wine Name ____________________

Winery ____________ Region ____________

Grapes ____________ Vintage ____________ Alcohol % ________

Appearance		☆ ☆ ☆ ☆ ☆
Aroma		☆ ☆ ☆ ☆ ☆
Body		☆ ☆ ☆ ☆ ☆
Taste		☆ ☆ ☆ ☆ ☆
Finish		☆ ☆ ☆ ☆ ☆

Pairs With	Serving Temperature

Notes

Ratings ☆ ☆ ☆ ☆ ☆

Wine Name ______________________

Winery ______________ Region ______________

Grapes ______________ Vintage ______________ Alcohol % ________

Appearance		☆ ☆ ☆ ☆ ☆
Aroma		☆ ☆ ☆ ☆ ☆
Body		☆ ☆ ☆ ☆ ☆
Taste		☆ ☆ ☆ ☆ ☆
Finish		☆ ☆ ☆ ☆ ☆

Pairs With	Serving Temperature

Notes

Ratings ☆ ☆ ☆ ☆ ☆

Wine Name

Winery ____________ Region ____________

Grapes ____________ Vintage ____________ Alcohol % ____________

Appearance		☆ ☆ ☆ ☆ ☆
Aroma		☆ ☆ ☆ ☆ ☆
Body		☆ ☆ ☆ ☆ ☆
Taste		☆ ☆ ☆ ☆ ☆
Finish		☆ ☆ ☆ ☆ ☆

Pairs With	Serving Temperature

Notes

Ratings ☆ ☆ ☆ ☆ ☆

Wine Name

Winery

Region

Grapes

Vintage

Alcohol %

Appearance		☆ ☆ ☆ ☆ ☆
Aroma		☆ ☆ ☆ ☆ ☆
Body		☆ ☆ ☆ ☆ ☆
Taste		☆ ☆ ☆ ☆ ☆
Finish		☆ ☆ ☆ ☆ ☆

Pairs With	Serving Temperature

Notes

Ratings ☆ ☆ ☆ ☆ ☆

Wine Name

Winery ______ Region ______

Grapes ______ Vintage ______ Alcohol % ______

Appearance		☆ ☆ ☆ ☆ ☆
Aroma		☆ ☆ ☆ ☆ ☆
Body		☆ ☆ ☆ ☆ ☆
Taste		☆ ☆ ☆ ☆ ☆
Finish		☆ ☆ ☆ ☆ ☆

Pairs With	Serving Temperature

Notes

Ratings ☆ ☆ ☆ ☆ ☆

Wine Name ______________________

Winery ______________ Region ______________

Grapes ______________ Vintage ______________ Alcohol % ________

Appearance		☆ ☆ ☆ ☆ ☆
Aroma		☆ ☆ ☆ ☆ ☆
Body		☆ ☆ ☆ ☆ ☆
Taste		☆ ☆ ☆ ☆ ☆
Finish		☆ ☆ ☆ ☆ ☆

Pairs With	Serving Temperature

Notes

Ratings ☆ ☆ ☆ ☆ ☆

Wine Name ____________________

Winery ____________ Region ____________

Grapes ____________ Vintage ____________ Alcohol % ________

Appearance		☆ ☆ ☆ ☆ ☆
Aroma		☆ ☆ ☆ ☆ ☆
Body		☆ ☆ ☆ ☆ ☆
Taste		☆ ☆ ☆ ☆ ☆
Finish		☆ ☆ ☆ ☆ ☆

Pairs With	Serving Temperature

Notes

Ratings ☆ ☆ ☆ ☆ ☆

Wine Name ____________________

Winery ____________________ Region ____________________

Grapes ____________________ Vintage ____________________ Alcohol % __________

Appearance		☆ ☆ ☆ ☆ ☆
Aroma		☆ ☆ ☆ ☆ ☆
Body		☆ ☆ ☆ ☆ ☆
Taste		☆ ☆ ☆ ☆ ☆
Finish		☆ ☆ ☆ ☆ ☆

Pairs With	Serving Temperature

Notes

Ratings ☆ ☆ ☆ ☆ ☆

Wine Name ____________________

Winery ____________ Region ____________

Grapes ____________ Vintage ____________ Alcohol % ________

Appearance		☆ ☆ ☆ ☆ ☆
Aroma		☆ ☆ ☆ ☆ ☆
Body		☆ ☆ ☆ ☆ ☆
Taste		☆ ☆ ☆ ☆ ☆
Finish		☆ ☆ ☆ ☆ ☆

Pairs With	Serving Temperature

Notes

Ratings ☆ ☆ ☆ ☆ ☆

Wine Name ______________________________

Winery ______________ Region ______________

Grapes ______________ Vintage ______________ Alcohol % ________

Appearance		☆ ☆ ☆ ☆ ☆
Aroma		☆ ☆ ☆ ☆ ☆
Body		☆ ☆ ☆ ☆ ☆
Taste		☆ ☆ ☆ ☆ ☆
Finish		☆ ☆ ☆ ☆ ☆

Pairs With	Serving Temperature

Notes

Ratings ☆ ☆ ☆ ☆ ☆

Wine Name ________________________

Winery ____________ Region ____________

Grapes ____________ Vintage ____________ Alcohol % ________

Appearance		☆ ☆ ☆ ☆ ☆
Aroma		☆ ☆ ☆ ☆ ☆
Body		☆ ☆ ☆ ☆ ☆
Taste		☆ ☆ ☆ ☆ ☆
Finish		☆ ☆ ☆ ☆ ☆

Pairs With	Serving Temperature

Notes

Ratings ☆ ☆ ☆ ☆ ☆

Wine Name ____________________

Winery ____________ Region ____________

Grapes ____________ Vintage ____________ Alcohol % ________

Appearance		☆ ☆ ☆ ☆ ☆
Aroma		☆ ☆ ☆ ☆ ☆
Body		☆ ☆ ☆ ☆ ☆
Taste		☆ ☆ ☆ ☆ ☆
Finish		☆ ☆ ☆ ☆ ☆

Pairs With	Serving Temperature

Notes

Ratings ☆ ☆ ☆ ☆ ☆

Wine Name ____________________

Winery ________ Region ________

Grapes ________ Vintage ________ Alcohol % ________

Appearance		☆ ☆ ☆ ☆ ☆
Aroma		☆ ☆ ☆ ☆ ☆
Body		☆ ☆ ☆ ☆ ☆
Taste		☆ ☆ ☆ ☆ ☆
Finish		☆ ☆ ☆ ☆ ☆

Pairs With	Serving Temperature

Notes

Ratings ☆ ☆ ☆ ☆ ☆

Wine Name

Winery ____ Region ____

Grapes ____ Vintage ____ Alcohol % ____

Appearance		☆ ☆ ☆ ☆ ☆
Aroma		☆ ☆ ☆ ☆ ☆
Body		☆ ☆ ☆ ☆ ☆
Taste		☆ ☆ ☆ ☆ ☆
Finish		☆ ☆ ☆ ☆ ☆

Pairs With	Serving Temperature

Notes

Ratings ☆ ☆ ☆ ☆ ☆

Wine Name ______________________

Winery ______________ Region ______________

Grapes ______________ Vintage ______________ Alcohol % ________

Appearance		☆ ☆ ☆ ☆ ☆
Aroma		☆ ☆ ☆ ☆ ☆
Body		☆ ☆ ☆ ☆ ☆
Taste		☆ ☆ ☆ ☆ ☆
Finish		☆ ☆ ☆ ☆ ☆

Pairs With	Serving Temperature

Notes

Ratings ☆ ☆ ☆ ☆ ☆

Wine Name ____________________

Winery ____________________ Region ____________________

Grapes ____________________ Vintage ____________________ Alcohol % __________

Appearance		☆ ☆ ☆ ☆ ☆
Aroma		☆ ☆ ☆ ☆ ☆
Body		☆ ☆ ☆ ☆ ☆
Taste		☆ ☆ ☆ ☆ ☆
Finish		☆ ☆ ☆ ☆ ☆

Pairs With	Serving Temperature

Notes

Ratings ☆ ☆ ☆ ☆ ☆

Wine Name ____________________

Winery ____________ Region ____________

Grapes ____________ Vintage ____________ Alcohol % ____________

Appearance		☆ ☆ ☆ ☆ ☆
Aroma		☆ ☆ ☆ ☆ ☆
Body		☆ ☆ ☆ ☆ ☆
Taste		☆ ☆ ☆ ☆ ☆
Finish		☆ ☆ ☆ ☆ ☆

Pairs With	Serving Temperature

Notes

Ratings ☆ ☆ ☆ ☆ ☆

Wine Name

Winery ______ Region ______

Grapes ______ Vintage ______ Alcohol % ______

Appearance		☆ ☆ ☆ ☆ ☆
Aroma		☆ ☆ ☆ ☆ ☆
Body		☆ ☆ ☆ ☆ ☆
Taste		☆ ☆ ☆ ☆ ☆
Finish		☆ ☆ ☆ ☆ ☆

Pairs With	Serving Temperature

Notes

Ratings ☆ ☆ ☆ ☆ ☆

Wine Name ____________________

Winery ____________ Region ____________

Grapes ____________ Vintage ____________ Alcohol % ________

Appearance		☆ ☆ ☆ ☆ ☆
Aroma		☆ ☆ ☆ ☆ ☆
Body		☆ ☆ ☆ ☆ ☆
Taste		☆ ☆ ☆ ☆ ☆
Finish		☆ ☆ ☆ ☆ ☆

Pairs With

Serving Temperature

Notes

Ratings ☆ ☆ ☆ ☆ ☆

Wine Name ______________________

Winery ______________ Region ______________

Grapes ______________ Vintage ______________ Alcohol % ________

Appearance		☆ ☆ ☆ ☆ ☆
Aroma		☆ ☆ ☆ ☆ ☆
Body		☆ ☆ ☆ ☆ ☆
Taste		☆ ☆ ☆ ☆ ☆
Finish		☆ ☆ ☆ ☆ ☆

Pairs With	Serving Temperature

Notes

Ratings ☆ ☆ ☆ ☆ ☆

Wine Name

Winery ____________ Region ____________

Grapes ____________ Vintage ____________ Alcohol % ____________

Appearance		☆ ☆ ☆ ☆ ☆
Aroma		☆ ☆ ☆ ☆ ☆
Body		☆ ☆ ☆ ☆ ☆
Taste		☆ ☆ ☆ ☆ ☆
Finish		☆ ☆ ☆ ☆ ☆

Pairs With	Serving Temperature

Notes

Ratings ☆ ☆ ☆ ☆ ☆

Wine Name

Winery ______ Region ______

Grapes ______ Vintage ______ Alcohol % ______

Appearance		☆ ☆ ☆ ☆ ☆
Aroma		☆ ☆ ☆ ☆ ☆
Body		☆ ☆ ☆ ☆ ☆
Taste		☆ ☆ ☆ ☆ ☆
Finish		☆ ☆ ☆ ☆ ☆

Pairs With	Serving Temperature

Notes

Ratings ☆ ☆ ☆ ☆ ☆

Wine Name ______________________

Winery ____________ Region ____________

Grapes ____________ Vintage ____________ Alcohol % ________

Appearance		☆ ☆ ☆ ☆ ☆
Aroma		☆ ☆ ☆ ☆ ☆
Body		☆ ☆ ☆ ☆ ☆
Taste		☆ ☆ ☆ ☆ ☆
Finish		☆ ☆ ☆ ☆ ☆

Pairs With	Serving Temperature

Notes

Ratings ☆ ☆ ☆ ☆ ☆

Wine Name ______________________

Winery ______________ Region ______________

Grapes ______________ Vintage ______________ Alcohol % ________

Appearance		☆ ☆ ☆ ☆ ☆
Aroma		☆ ☆ ☆ ☆ ☆
Body		☆ ☆ ☆ ☆ ☆
Taste		☆ ☆ ☆ ☆ ☆
Finish		☆ ☆ ☆ ☆ ☆

Pairs With	Serving Temperature

Notes

Ratings ☆ ☆ ☆ ☆ ☆

Wine Name ____________________

Winery ____________ Region ____________

Grapes ____________ Vintage ____________ Alcohol % ________

Appearance		☆ ☆ ☆ ☆ ☆
Aroma		☆ ☆ ☆ ☆ ☆
Body		☆ ☆ ☆ ☆ ☆
Taste		☆ ☆ ☆ ☆ ☆
Finish		☆ ☆ ☆ ☆ ☆

Pairs With	Serving Temperature

Notes

Ratings ☆ ☆ ☆ ☆ ☆

Wine Name ______________________

Winery ____________ Region ____________

Grapes ____________ Vintage ____________ Alcohol % ________

Appearance		☆ ☆ ☆ ☆ ☆
Aroma		☆ ☆ ☆ ☆ ☆
Body		☆ ☆ ☆ ☆ ☆
Taste		☆ ☆ ☆ ☆ ☆
Finish		☆ ☆ ☆ ☆ ☆

Pairs With	Serving Temperature

Notes

Ratings ☆ ☆ ☆ ☆ ☆

Wine Name

Winery

Region

Grapes

Vintage

Alcohol %

Appearance		☆ ☆ ☆ ☆ ☆
Aroma		☆ ☆ ☆ ☆ ☆
Body		☆ ☆ ☆ ☆ ☆
Taste		☆ ☆ ☆ ☆ ☆
Finish		☆ ☆ ☆ ☆ ☆

Pairs With

Serving Temperature

Notes

Ratings ☆ ☆ ☆ ☆ ☆

Wine Name

Winery ______ Region ______

Grapes ______ Vintage ______ Alcohol % ______

Appearance		☆ ☆ ☆ ☆ ☆
Aroma		☆ ☆ ☆ ☆ ☆
Body		☆ ☆ ☆ ☆ ☆
Taste		☆ ☆ ☆ ☆ ☆
Finish		☆ ☆ ☆ ☆ ☆

Pairs With	Serving Temperature

Notes

Ratings ☆ ☆ ☆ ☆ ☆

Wine Name

Winery ____________ Region ____________

Grapes ____________ Vintage ____________ Alcohol % ____________

Appearance		☆ ☆ ☆ ☆ ☆
Aroma		☆ ☆ ☆ ☆ ☆
Body		☆ ☆ ☆ ☆ ☆
Taste		☆ ☆ ☆ ☆ ☆
Finish		☆ ☆ ☆ ☆ ☆

Pairs With	Serving Temperature

Notes

Ratings ☆ ☆ ☆ ☆ ☆

Wine Name

Winery Region

Grapes Vintage Alcohol %

Appearance		☆ ☆ ☆ ☆ ☆
Aroma		☆ ☆ ☆ ☆ ☆
Body		☆ ☆ ☆ ☆ ☆
Taste		☆ ☆ ☆ ☆ ☆
Finish		☆ ☆ ☆ ☆ ☆

Pairs With	Serving Temperature

Notes

Ratings ☆ ☆ ☆ ☆ ☆

Wine Name ______

Winery ______ Region ______

Grapes ______ Vintage ______ Alcohol % ______

Appearance		☆ ☆ ☆ ☆ ☆
Aroma		☆ ☆ ☆ ☆ ☆
Body		☆ ☆ ☆ ☆ ☆
Taste		☆ ☆ ☆ ☆ ☆
Finish		☆ ☆ ☆ ☆ ☆

Pairs With	Serving Temperature

Notes

Ratings ☆ ☆ ☆ ☆ ☆

Wine Name ____________________

Winery ____________ Region ____________

Grapes ____________ Vintage ____________ Alcohol % ________

Appearance		☆ ☆ ☆ ☆ ☆
Aroma		☆ ☆ ☆ ☆ ☆
Body		☆ ☆ ☆ ☆ ☆
Taste		☆ ☆ ☆ ☆ ☆
Finish		☆ ☆ ☆ ☆ ☆

Pairs With	Serving Temperature

Notes

Ratings ☆ ☆ ☆ ☆ ☆

Made in the USA
Thornton, CO
12/17/22 19:04:55

47a87dc0-1f1c-49db-844d-f91938a93a6bR01